THE DEPARTMENT OF

HOMELAND SECURITY

A LOOK BEHIND THE SCENES

By Karen Latchana Kenney

Content Consultant:
Brian Nussbaum, PhD
Assistant Professor
University at Albany
Albany, New York

COMPASS POINT BOOKS
a capstone imprint

Compass Point Books are published by Capstone
1710 Roe Crest Drive, North Mankato, Minnesota 56003
www.mycapstone.com

Library of Congress Cataloging-in-Publication Data
Names: Kenney, Karen Latchana.
Title: The Department of Homeland Security : a look behind the scenes / by Karen Latchana Kenney.
Description: North Mankato, Minnesota : Compass Point Books, [2019] | Series: U.S. government behind the scenes | Audience: Ages 12-17. | Includes bibliographical references and index.
Identifiers: LCCN 2018042023 (print) | LCCN 2018049483 (ebook) | ISBN 9780756559144 (ebook PDF) | ISBN 9780756559014 (hardcover) | ISBN 9780756559106 (pbk.)
Subjects: LCSH: United States. Department of Homeland Security—Juvenile literature. | Terrorism—United States—Prevention—Juvenile literature. | National security—United States—Juvenile literature.
Classification: LCC HV6432.4 (ebook) | LCC HV6432.4 .K46 2019 (print) | DDC 363.340973—dc23
LC record available at https://lccn.loc.gov/2018042023

Editorial Credits:
Amy Kortuem, editor; Terri Poburka, designer; Jo Miller, media researcher Tori Abraham, production specialist

Image Credits:
Department of Homeland Security, 55; Getty Images: Alex Wong/Staff, 46, David Pollack/Contributor, 20, Hero Images, 57, Joshua Roberts/Staff, 33, Kyodo News/Contributor, 5 (bottom), MCT/Contributor, 35, Tim Boyle/Staff, 29; Newscom: akg-images, 19, KRT/John Fitzhugh, 6, KRT/Lindeman, 40, Reuters/Hugh Gentry, 5 (top), Reuters/Larry Downing, 27, 31, 53, Reuters/STR, 25, Richard B. Levine, 44, TNS/Nelvin C. Cepeda, 9, UPI Photo Service/Mike Hvozda/USCG Photo, 39, ZUMA Press/Carter Archives, 22, ZUMA Press/Jocelyn Augustino, 42, ZUMA Press/K.C. Alfred, 51; Shutterstock: Diego G Diaz, 49, KENRICK GRIFFITH, Cover; Wikimedia: Harris and Ewing, 15, Jud McCranie, 10, NARA, 17

Design Elements:
Shutterstock: anndypit, ben Bryant, RetroClipArt, Tobias Steinert

Printed and bound in the USA.
PA49

TABLE OF CONTENTS

CHAPTER ONE

Emergency Alert!

At 8:07 a.m. on January 13, 2018, an urgent alert went out to cellphones across Hawaii. This text message read, "BALLISTIC MISSILE THREAT INBOUND TO HAWAII. SEEK IMMEDIATE SHELTER. THIS IS NOT A DRILL." Another message ran across the bottom of television screens: "If you are outdoors, seek immediate shelter in a building. Remain indoors well away from windows. If you are driving, pull safely to the side of the road and seek shelter in a nearby building or lie on the floor. We will announce when the threat has ended."

The state had been doing monthly drills for a situation like this. A nuclear attack was on people's minds. U.S. President Donald Trump and North Korean dictator Kim Jong Un had been trading nuclear threats with each other. Earlier in the month, Kim stated that "a nuclear button is always on my desk [and the] entire United States is within range of our nuclear weapons." Guam, Alaska, and Hawaii were the closest targets that North Korea could hit if it decided to attack the United States. It would take less than 30 minutes for a missile to reach Hawaii from North Korea. Hawaiian officials had warned residents to find shelter within 12 minutes of a missile alert.

People panicked. Where could they take shelter from a nuclear missile? Some people were driving when they got the message. They parked their cars inside a highway tunnel through a mountain. State representative Matt LoPresti hid in his bathroom. He said, “I was sitting in the bathtub with my children, saying our prayers.” Some families hid in their closets or basements. At Konawaena High School, the alert came during a wrestling championship. School officials moved everyone to the middle of the gym.

The threat terrified many people across the state, but it turned out to be a mistake. Thirty-eight minutes after it went out, Hawaiians received a new message stating that there was no threat.

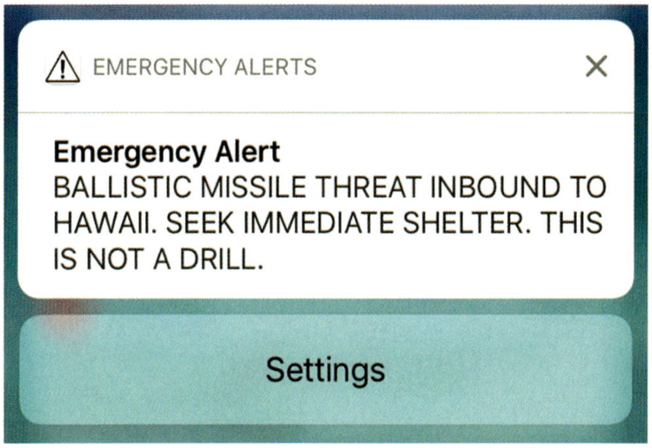

Kim Jong Un has served as the leader of North Korea since 2011.

FEMA is the agency of the Department of Homeland Security tasked with helping people before, during, and after disasters.

What happened? A warning officer at the Hawaii Emergency Management Agency misunderstood that the alert he was supposed to send out was a drill. He thought it was a real attack warning.

While the alert that day in Hawaii was a false alarm, the system did what it was meant to do. What if a missile had been heading toward the state at that moment? That alert might have saved lives. This alert was a Civil Danger Warning, one kind of message that is sent out through the Integrated Public Alert and Warning System (IPAWS). This system quickly warns citizens of emergencies, such as missile threats or hurricanes, through messages on cellphones, radios, and televisions. States use this federal system to send out local emergency alerts to their residents. This system is acted out at the federal level in part by the Federal Emergency Management Agency (FEMA). FEMA is one of 22 agencies of the Department of Homeland Security (DHS).

Inside the Department of Homeland Security

The U.S. government is split into three branches: the executive, the judicial, and the legislative. The executive branch carries out and enforces laws. It includes the president, the vice president, the cabinet, and departments, along with other agencies, committees, commissions, and boards. The Department of Homeland Security is one of the 15 departments within the executive branch. It is the third largest of the group. The largest is the Department of Defense. The second largest is the Department of Veteran Affairs. Other departments in the government are the Department of Agriculture, Department of State, the Department of Education.

Currently at the head of the Department of Homeland Security is Secretary Kirstjen M. Nielsen. Nielsen is a former DHS employee. She was appointed to the top position by President Donald Trump and confirmed by the Senate. This is the procedure for all appointees. As the DHS secretary, Nielsen also sits on the cabinet, a group of advisors to the president. She leads 240,000 people in a department made up of 22 different components, from the U.S. Coast Guard to the Secret Service and the Transportation Security Administration. The department's goal is to keep the United States and its citizens safe from attack, threat, and disaster.

The 22 components of the Department of Homeland Security protect the United States in very different ways. The Office of the Secretary runs the Department of Homeland Security. Within it are 10 offices with various duties. One is the Office for Civil Rights and Civil Liberties, which works to preserve, defend, and promote civil rights and liberties in the United States. Another, the Office of the Citizenship and Immigration Services Ombudsman, focuses on improving citizenship and immigration services.

Several parts of DHS work to secure the borders from illegal flows of goods and people, including drugs, illegal immigration, human trafficking, and terrorists. They include the U.S. Customs and Border Protection; Immigration and Customs Enforcement (ICE); and The United States Citizenship and Immigration Services. Many of these divisions work to stop terrorists from entering the country or to stop terrorist acts from happening. In 2017 Nielsen created a new group focused just on terrorist weapons and counterterrorism. It is the Countering Weapons of Mass Destruction office. This office works to prevent terrorists from using chemical, nuclear, and other kinds of weapons to harm people in the United States.

FEMA coordinates federal responses to different kinds of disasters that affect people in the United States—from terrorist attacks to floods and hurricanes. Its biggest duty is to organize the delivery of food, water, emergency shelter, and other aid to disaster victims in need of help.

President Donald Trump appointed Kirstjen Nielsen secretary of DHS in 2017.

FLETC's mission is to train all those who protect the United States, including state, local, and tribal departments.

The Federal Law Enforcement Training Center (FLETC) operates federal training centers for people in law enforcement. Other offices provide technology and information to the heads of the department.

The Department of Homeland Security has five main security-focused missions. First, the DHS focuses on counterterrorism by working to prevent terrorist attacks and the transportation of bomb-making materials within the United States. It makes sure the country's infrastructure—its systems of transportation, communication, power plants, and schools—are protected from attack. Second, the department works to secure the country's air, land, and sea borders by patrolling and guarding the borders, monitoring trade and travel, and finding and breaking apart terrorist and criminal organizations and their activities. Third, the DHS oversees immigration policy. It enforces immigration laws, grants citizenship to immigrants who arrive through proper channels, and finds and deports undocumented immigrants. Fourth, the department is responsible for cyberspace security. The department works to keep government computer systems safe from hackers and cyberattacks. Fifth, the DHS helps Americans recover from large-scale emergencies and disasters through FEMA.

This vast department's responsibilities aim to protect the United States in a multitude of ways. Before DHS was founded, many of these responsibilities were undertaken by civil defense agencies within federal and state governments. Pulling together federal efforts in these areas under the umbrella of one department was the federal government's most dramatic reorganization. This need for a unified civil defense department evolved along with technological advances and new threats to the United States throughout its history. The terrorist attacks of September 2001 solidified the urgent need for a Department of Homeland Security.

A Real Emergency Alert

What if a missile really had been heading toward Hawaii on January 13, 2018? What would have happened to alert the public to the dangerous situation? First, infrared satellites orbiting Earth would detect the heat created by a ballistic missile launching into the air. The satellites would immediately relay that information to the military and analysts would figure out what kind of missile was launched and where it was headed. Then the U.S. Northern Command, the part of the military responsible for protecting the homeland, would discuss the situation with U.S. Pacific Command and U.S. Strategic Command and decide on a response. The command groups would then contact FEMA and it would make a secure call to the Hawaiian Emergency Management Agency. The authorities there would send an emergency message back to FEMA and it would distribute the message through the Integrated Public Alert & Warning System (IPAWS). The alert would then instantly appear on all cellphones, digital billboards, road signs, televisions, and other notification systems in Hawaii.

Organization Chart of the U.S. Department of Homeland Security

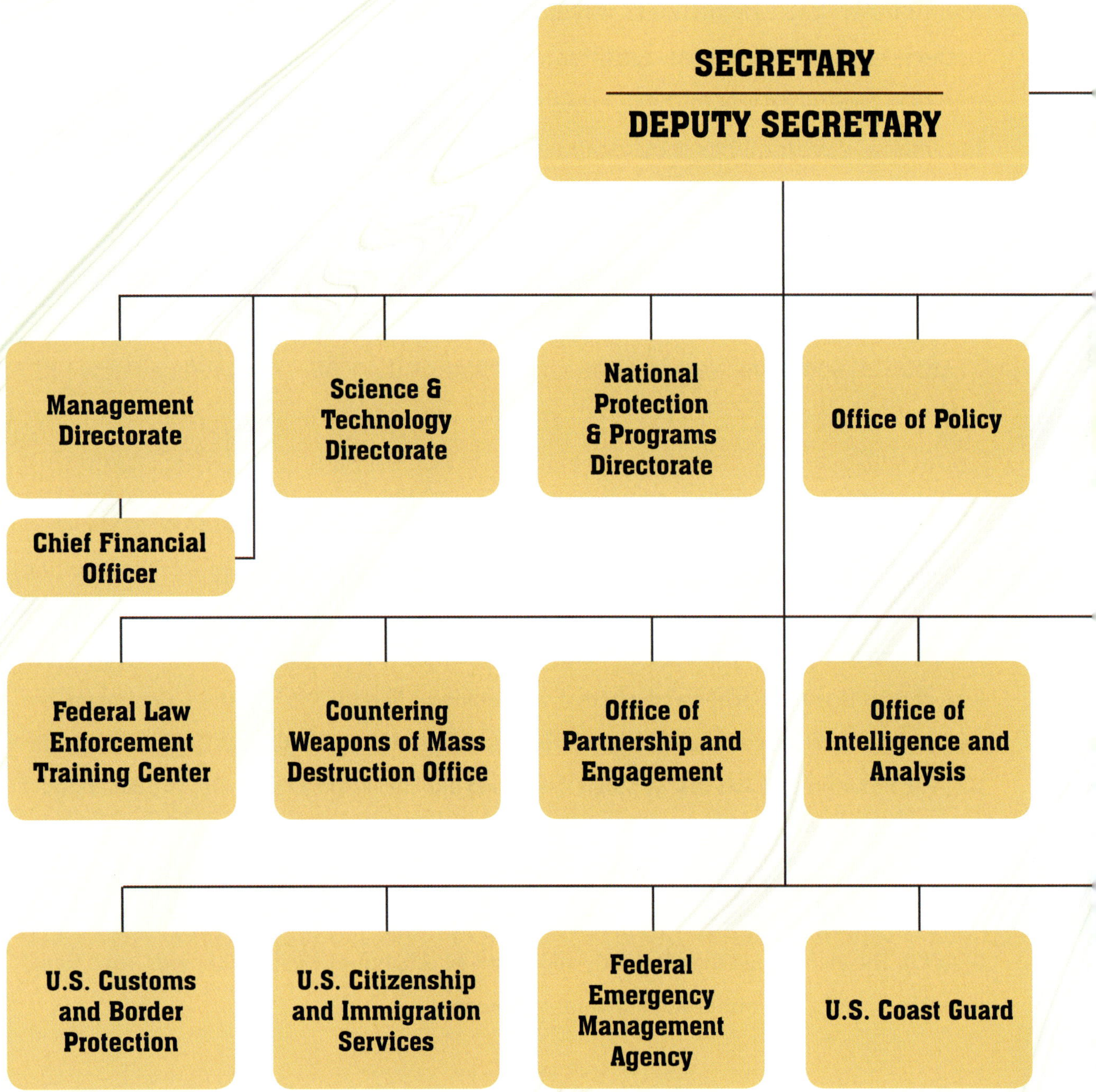

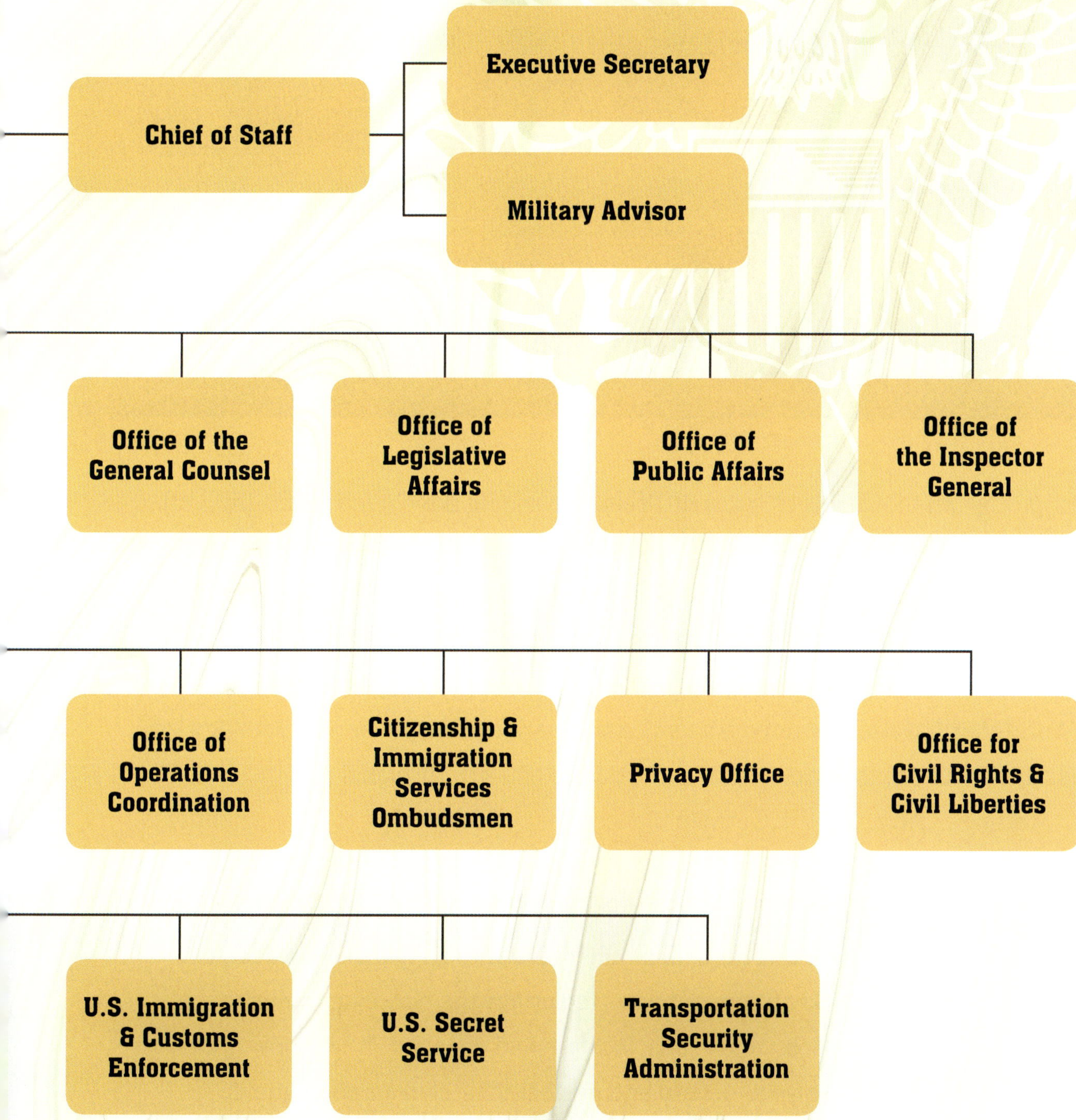
Chief of Staff
Executive Secretary
Military Advisor
Office of the General Counsel
Office of Legislative Affairs
Office of Public Affairs
Office of the Inspector General
Office of Operations Coordination
Citizenship & Immigration Services Ombudsmen
Privacy Office
Office for Civil Rights & Civil Liberties
U.S. Immigration & Customs Enforcement
U.S. Secret Service
Transportation Security Administration

CHAPTER TWO

Needing Civil Defense

With thousands of miles of ocean separating the United States from other nations with advanced weaponry, there was little need for a federal civil defense program before World War I (1914–1918). The U.S. government did not fear a sudden major attack from any country. The U.S. was simply too far away from Russia and other armed countries for that to happen. But at the start of World War I, warfare entered a new phase. There was now a new technology countries could use to attack towns and cities by air—the airplane.

Starting in August 1914, German planes bombed towns and cities in countries across Europe, including Belgium, England, and France. Warfare moved from remote battlefields to areas where thousands or even millions of civilians lived. The nations were unprepared for these attacks against their civilians. They lacked evacuation plans. People had to quickly figure out ways to survive the bombings, which destroyed buildings, services, and roads. Warfare had changed. It was now necessary for countries to provide ways to defend and protect their civilian populations.

The United States established its first civil defense program in 1916. Called the Council of National Defense (CND), it focused on gathering the country's resources in support of the war effort. The council's members included secretaries from the War, Navy, Commerce, Interior, Agriculture, and Labor departments. Its duty was to advise the president on how to mobilize resources, such as food and medical supplies, if the country entered the war abroad. Local civil defense programs formed in states to help the national effort. But a few years after the war ended in 1918, the Council of National Defense and local civil defense programs disbanded.

The Council of National Defense was established during President Woodrow Wilson's administration. It was led by Grosvenor B. Clarkson (left).

In the 1930s war was again brewing in Europe. Nations began stockpiling weapons in preparation. Out of concern for what was happening there, and the possible involvement of the United States, President Franklin Roosevelt ordered the creation of the National Emergency Council in 1933. Part of its duties was to coordinate national emergency programs. Civil defense efforts were also coordinated at the state and local level across the United States.

Then World War II (1939–1945) broke out in Europe as the Germans sought to control the continent. President Roosevelt reestablished the CND in 1940 under the new name: the National Defense Research Committee. Local programs formed again to prepare the country for war. But now people were afraid the U.S. homeland was going to be attacked too. New York City Mayor Fiorello La Guardia wrote to Roosevelt about his concerns for U.S. civilian safety and the need for a strong federal civil defense program: "Never in our history has the civilian population been exposed to attack. The new technique of war has created the necessity for developing new techniques of civilian defense."

In response to the rising concerns from officials, Roosevelt created the Office of Civilian Defense (OCD) in 1941. It coordinated the efforts of local civil defense offices around the country. Many relied on volunteers to carry out OCD duties. They included drivers, emergency rescuers, and voluntary police and bomb squad workers. The OCD told citizens what to do during air raids. It supervised blackouts to protect cities against air raids. It also planned how to fight fires in case of an attack. A little more than six months after the OCD was established, Americans' fears came true when Japan attacked by air. The bombing of Pearl Harbor was a wake-up call. The United States was not safe from an attack against its homeland. But after the war ended, the office was not needed any more because the threat of attack was gone. President Harry S. Truman issued an executive order removing the OCD on June 4, 1945.

New York City Mayor La Guardia (left) urged President Roosevelt (right) to create a civil defense program.

Defense in the Atomic Age

The development of the atomic bomb posed a new threat, though. The United States dropped two atomic bombs in Japan near the end of World War II. The bomb devastated the cities of Nagasaki and Hiroshima. Soon the Soviet Union and other countries were racing to develop their own nuclear weapons. The United States and the Soviet Union were becoming increasingly hostile to one another. Then the Soviets successfully tested a nuclear weapon in August 1949. The threat of a nuclear attack on U.S. soil was now real. The American public, local officials, and Congress wanted the U.S. government to have a civil defense plan.

Truman and others in the federal government believed that state and local governments should carry out most of the duties of civil defense. In 1951 Truman created the Federal Civil Defense Administration (FCDA). Truman said the law afforded "the basic framework for preparations to minimize the effects of an attack on our civilian population, and to deal with the immediate emergency conditions which such an attack would create."

The FCDA provided guidance and grants to state and local governments in their civil defense efforts. It designed bomb shelters to protect people during an atomic blast. It led public education programs telling people what to do if they saw an atomic blast. As it evolved, the FCDA moved from promoting shelters to mass evacuation plans, as the harmful health effects of nuclear bombing and radiation became known.

Yet many believed civil defense should focus on shelters, and they criticized President Dwight D. Eisenhower and the FCDA. Eisenhower dissolved it and established the Office of Civil and Defense Mobilization (OCDM) in 1958. It merged the FCDA with the Office of Defense Mobilization (ODM). In 1961 new president John F. Kennedy split the OCDM into two offices: the Office of Emergency Planning and the Office of Civil Defense (OCD). Civil defense remained focused on preparing and responding to nuclear bombings throughout Kennedy's presidency and into that of the next president, Lyndon B. Johnson.

Duck and Cover

In the early 1950s, millions of children across the United States watched a cartoon movie in their classrooms and on television. Titled *Duck and Cover*, it had cute, friendly looking illustrations and a cheerful song. The movie began with Bert the Turtle taking a stroll through the woods. When Bert sees a monkey hanging from a tree holding a lit stick of dynamite, he reacts. Bert quickly pulls inside his shell to avoid the blasting dynamite. The peppy song lyrics told Bert's story:

"There was a turtle by the name of Bert
and Bert the turtle was very alert;
when danger threatened him he never got hurt.
He knew just what to do.
He'd duck! And cover! Duck! And cover!
He did what we all must learn to do.
You and you and you and you!
Duck, and cover!"

Drawings such as this 1951 example were meant to prepare students for possible attacks.

The film was one of nine made by the FCDA, which were shown to children in schools as part of a public education campaign. The movies told children what to do in case of an atomic bomb explosion in their area. Just like Bert the Turtle, the children were instructed to duck under their desks, crouch with their heads facing down, and cover their necks so they wouldn't be hurt by the blast. The film taught children that an atomic bomb blast was a danger Americans had to be prepared for, just like learning what to do in case of a fire. It described what would happen during an atomic blast and warned that, without preparation, they could be seriously injured. Although the FCDA promoted this "duck and cover" technique, it would have done nothing to protect anyone from the effects of a nuclear blast. At the time, the long-lasting, cancer-causing effects of radioactivity resulting from a nuclear explosion were not widely known.

The Federal Civil Defense Administration created posters showing a nuclear bomb to recruit members.

Responding to Disasters

For the next decade, the OCD—and with it, national civil defense—was at a standstill. Some major natural disasters hit the country in 1964 and 1965. A 9.2 magnitude Alaskan earthquake in 1964 caused a tsunami wave that devastated parts of Alaska, California, and British Columbia, Canada. Two hurricanes struck the southeast hard: Hurricane Hilda and Hurricane Betsy. Then on April 11, 1965, 47 deadly tornadoes swept across six states in the Midwest, leaving a path of destruction behind them. More than 1,500 people were injured and 271 people died. After this series of disasters, Senator Birch Bayh of Indiana sponsored a bill to provide emergency federal funds to victims of the disasters. It passed in 1966. Bayh suggested more assistance be offered in the future.

Historically, Congress had waited until after disasters happened to organize a response. This was beginning to change. Disaster assistance would become a focus for future legislators. President Richard Nixon replaced the OCD with the Defense Civil Preparedness Agency (DCPA) in 1972. It included funding for civil defense and natural disaster preparedness. Later, Nixon began reorganizing civil defense duties, spreading them across different agencies.

On March 28, 1979, the Three Mile Island accident happened near Harrisburg, Pennsylvania. This nuclear power plant failed to operate properly and overheated, releasing radioactive material. It was the worst nuclear power plant accident in U.S. history. Evacuation plans weren't handled properly. The information reported by officials kept changing. This accident revealed that the government needed a better way to respond to a disaster. On April 1, 1979, President Jimmy Carter established the Federal Emergency Management Agency (FEMA). It became the central agency for coordinating federal disaster response and relief efforts.

President Jimmy Carter (light gray suit) and his wife, Rosalynn Carter, toured the Three Mile Island nuclear power plant after the accident in 1979.

The New Threat: Terrorism

FEMA grew and developed, but a new threat began to emerge. On February 26, 1993, an act of terrorism took the United States by surprise. Two men parked a yellow truck in the parking lot under the World Trade Center in New York City and set off a half-ton bomb. The explosion didn't topple the towers, but it did fill them with smoke and cut off the electricity. Six people died and thousands were injured. The drivers were jihadist terrorists who were against U.S. involvement in the Middle East and its support of Israel.

Throughout 1995 and 1996, more terrorist attacks occurred around the world and in the United States. Terrorists released poisonous gas in Tokyo subways. Other terrorists bombed a U.S. military building in Saudi Arabia. Then in 1995 Timothy McVeigh and Terry Nichols bombed the Alfred P. Murrah Federal Building in Oklahoma City, Oklahoma. The federal government now felt it needed to defend the country's citizens against terrorist acts. In 1998 President Bill Clinton enacted the Office of the National Coordinator for Security, Infrastructure Protection, and Counter-Terrorism. Shortly after President George W. Bush took office in 2001, a new terrorist act of unimaginable scale made protecting the homeland the most important issue facing the country.

CHAPTER THREE

The Birth of the Department

When Americans turned on their televisions to watch the morning news on September 11, 2001, what they saw on their screens seemed straight out of a disaster movie. But it was real. New Yorkers were experiencing it right at that moment. Viewers watched the live footage of the World Trade Center's north tower in the financial district of New York City. It was on fire and billowing smoke from the top part of the building. A plane had crashed into it, but the reporters did not know if it was an accident—no one knew what had happened.

Then, as this live footage rolled, a second passenger airplane flew straight into the south tower of the World Trade Center. It was now obvious that these crashes were not accidents. This was a planned attack against the towers, two famous landmarks of the New York City skyline and symbols of U.S. strength and power.

Both towers of the World Trade Center collapsed after terrorists attacked them on September 11, 2001.

New Yorkers tried to evacuate the area as fast as they could. Firefighters, police officers, and other emergency workers rushed to the scene to try and save the people stuck inside the burning and collapsing buildings. People across the United States watched the events on live television in shock. They would soon learn that terrorists had hijacked two more airplanes. The terrorists crashed one into the Pentagon, home of the Department of Defense. Another airplane crashed into a field in southern Pennsylvania. It was believed to be headed to the U.S. Capitol or the White House, but some passengers overtook the terrorists and blocked their plans.

How could this kind of organized attack happen in America? How did the terrorists and their plans go unnoticed? Who would use passenger airplanes as guided missiles to destroy skyscrapers and government buildings filled with people starting their workday on a Tuesday morning? Americans had many unanswered questions. But one thing was certain from the first moments of what came to be called the 9/11 tragedy. The United States of America and its people would never be the same. This event would forever change the nation.

On the night of September 11 President Bush addressed a fearful, angry, and sad nation on TV. He assured Americans that their country was strong and that this tragedy would not break the American spirit. He said, "America was targeted for attack because we're the brightest beacon for freedom and opportunity in the world. And no one will keep that light from shining. Today our nation saw evil, the very worst of human nature. And we responded with the best of America, with the daring of our rescue workers, with the caring for strangers and neighbors who came to give blood and help in any way they could." President Bush vowed to find the terrorists. "The search is underway for those who are behind these evil acts," he said. "I've directed the full resources of our intelligence and law enforcement communities to find those responsible and to bring them to justice. We will make no distinction between the terrorists who committed these acts and those who harbor them."

President George W. Bush addressed the nation on the evening of the 9/11 attacks.

Americans later learned that 19 jihadist terrorists had acted that day on a plan that had been years in the making. Leaders of the jihadist extremist group al-Qaeda in Afghanistan had coordinated the attacks. Some of the young men who carried out the attacks had been in the United States for more than a year. Four trained as pilots and had studied the weaknesses of U.S. airport security. They made their way through security on September 11 carrying box cutters, small knives, and cans of mace and pepper spray. The terrorists overcame the flight staff and pilots with these weapons and took over flying the planes. They killed nearly 2,700 people at the World Trade Center, more than 100 people at the Pentagon, and 265 people on the planes.

Taking Immediate Action: Post-9/11

In the days after 9/11, the Bush administration took immediate action. It began reviewing a number of problems that needed to be resolved. These included finding out the amount of federal assistance that was needed in New York City, starting air travel again with increased security, and returning port and border security to normal operations. Different government agencies were responsible for disaster response, aviation security, and controlling the people and goods crossing borders. No central department controlled the security of the nation. Three days after the terrorist attacks, Vice President Dick Cheney recommended the creation of a new White House department to coordinate the different agencies. On October 8, 2001, President Bush created the Office of Homeland Security as part of his cabinet, with a homeland security advisor. The first advisor was Pennsylvania governor Tom Ridge.

On September 10, 2002, 500 federally trained security workers took over the passenger screening work at Chicago's O'Hare airport.

Then the first legislation to pass in response to the 9/11 attacks became law on November 19, 2001. It focused on increasing the security of U.S. airports and airplanes. The Aviation and Transportation Security Act authorized the creation of a new federal agency called the Transportation Security Administration (TSA) under the Department of Transportation.

Before the creation of the TSA, airports hired security screeners from different private companies. They followed Federal Aviation Administration (FAA) rules, which allowed passengers to carry box cutters, knives up to 4 inches (10 cm) long, baseball bats, knitting needles, scissors, and more. After TSA was created, these items and others were banned. Transportation security was now under federal control. All screeners had to be federal employees of the TSA. The Aviation and Transportation Security Act also required reinforced cockpit doors in airplanes and expanded the Federal Air Marshal Service. Federal air marshals are law enforcement officers who travel on airplanes in civilian clothes. Passengers do not know they are air marshals. The air marshals carry guns and are trained to take down a terrorist inside an airplane. Before 9/11, there were 33 air marshals covering all of the U.S. flights. By 2005 more than 5,000 were on the job.

Establishing the TSA and addressing vulnerabilities in airports and on airplanes was the first of many government actions that happened quickly after 9/11. More than 130 pieces of legislation related to 9/11 passed in the following year. One major and controversial act quickly became law on October 26, 2001. The USA PATRIOT Act gave law enforcement agencies more surveillance powers in their search for terrorists. It also required different agencies to share more information between them, something they hadn't been doing pre–9/11. The FAA, FBI, and CIA all had different watch lists—lists of suspects the agencies were looking for or didn't want to let into the country. The fact that there were different watch lists on the morning of 9/11 highlighted the need for the sharing of important information between agencies.

The FAA, responsible for air safety, only had 12 people on its watch list, which was provided to airlines. If a passenger was on the list, that person could not board an airplane. The CIA and FBI had hundreds more names on their watch lists, but these names were not on the FAA's list. It was later revealed that two of the hijackers' names had been on the FBI and CIA lists. It was clear that the agencies needed to share their information to better protect the airlines and terrorist investigations. The government was taking steps toward securing the United States' borders, safeguarding air travel better, and finding terrorists. One of the biggest steps was yet to happen.

President Bush signed the Secure Transportation and Aviation Act at Reagan National Airport in November 2001.

Reorganizing the Government

President Bush began laying the foundations for a new Department of Homeland Security in January 2002. In his State of the Union address, he introduced the USA Freedom Corps. These voluntary groups of citizens could receive training and support so they would be able to prevent, protect, respond, and recover from hazards, whether related to terrorism or not. Then in March, the Homeland Security Advisory System (HSAS) was created. This color-coded system communicated the threat level of a terrorist attack to the public. The system went from red (the most severe threat level) to green (the lowest threat level).

Bush issued an executive order in March for a Homeland Security Advisory Council within the White House to advise him on homeland security issues. The president and his administration also began working on a strategy for the nation's homeland security. As they were doing so, Congress was pushing for a reorganization of the government departments and agencies involved with different aspects of homeland security. These duties were spread among more than 100 different government organizations. America required a single homeland security department that would improve protection against current and future threats. President Bush then submitted his plan for the creation of a Department of Homeland Security in June 2002.

The plan listed four main divisions of the department: Border and Transportation Security; Emergency Preparedness and Response; Chemical, Biological, Radiological and Nuclear Countermeasures (to prepare and plan for state and national responses to terrorist threats and attacks); and Information Analysis and Infrastructure Protection (to merge and analyze intelligence from various agencies, including the FBI and CIA, issue warnings to the public, and determine risks to infrastructure). This department would work to prevent terrorist attacks, make the United States less vulnerable to attacks, and lessen the damage and recovery time from attacks that happened. The plan also listed which departments and agencies would be reorganized into the new department.

In November 2002 the Homeland Security Act passed in Congress. Bush signed it into law on November 25, establishing the new Department of Homeland Security. This pulling together of various agencies and departments was the biggest government reorganization since the 1940s. President Bush appointed his Homeland Security advisor, Tom Ridge, as its very first secretary. Ridge left the White House cabinet to head up the enormous job of creating a new government department.

DHS Secretary Tom Ridge described the department's new color-coded threat advisory system.

Attacking America: al-Qaeda

The radical Islamic terrorist group that planned and executed the attack against the Twin Towers on September 11, 2001, was al-Qaeda. It began in the 1980s when its leader, Osama bin Laden, fought against the Soviet Union in Afghanistan. In 1996 bin Laden was living in Afghanistan and publicly declared war against America. He was opposed to U.S. troops being in Saudi Arabia, his homeland, and to the U.S.-Israel alliance. He was also opposed to U.S. policies in the Middle East and South Asia. Osama bin Laden believed that what he called the "Jewish-Christian" alliance had imposed aggression and injustice on the people of Islam.

Others who agreed with bin Laden's extremist views joined al-Qaeda. They believed in its mission to fight, kill, and destroy Americans. Its members were willing to commit suicide to successfully attack and kill Americans. Al-Qaeda carried out its first major attack against the United States in 1998 when it bombed U.S. embassies in Kenya and Tanzania and killed 224 people, including 12 Americans. In 2000 the group attacked the *USS Cole*, a U.S. destroyer warship, and killed 17 people. Then in 2001 al-Qaeda succeeded in attacking New York City, killing close to 3,000 people.

After 9/11, the United States invaded Afghanistan in an attempt to stop al-Qaeda. President Bush declared a "war against terrorism." Troops fought to destroy al-Qaeda training camps and shut down the Taliban forces that had hosted them. The war did not completely destroy al-Qaeda, but no other terrorist attack on the scale of 9/11 has happened since. Bin Laden remained in hiding, leading al-Qaeda from unknown locations. Eventually U.S. intelligence agencies found him. On May 2, 2011, during the administration of President Barack Obama, U.S. Special Forces killed bin Laden in Pakistan. After bin Laden's death, al-Qaeda lost some of the strength it once had. But it still exists and has groups in several countries. Al-Qaeda and the groups it is linked to are some of the terrorist organizations monitored by the U.S. government around the world.

Vice President Joe Biden (left), President Barack Obama (second from left), and members of the national security team waited to hear the fate of Osama bin Laden after U.S. Special Forces attacked the al-Qaeda leader's compound in 2011.

9/11: Minute-by-Minute

7:59 a.m.
American Airlines Flight 11 takes off from Boston with 92 people on board.

8:14 a.m.
United Airlines Flight 175 takes off from Boston with 65 people on board.

8:20 a.m.
American Airlines Flight 77 takes off from Washington, D.C., with 64 people on board.

8:40 a.m.
The FAA suspects Flight 11 has been hijacked and informs the military.

8:41 a.m.
United Airlines Flight 93 takes off from Newark with 44 people on board.

8:43 a.m.
The FAA suspects Flight 175 has been hijacked and informs the military.

8:46 a.m.
Flight 11 crashes into the North Tower of the World Trade Center.

9:03 a.m.
Flight 175 crashes into the South Tower of the World Trade Center.

9:24 a.m.
The FAA suspects Flight 77 has been hijacked and informs the military.

9:26 a.m.
The FAA bans all aircraft in the country from taking off.

9:37 a.m.
Flight 77 crashes into the Pentagon.

9:42 a.m.
The FAA grounds all aircraft for the first time in U.S. history.

9:59 a.m.
The South Tower of the World Trade Center collapses, crashing to the ground.

10:07 a.m.
Flight 93 crashes in a field near Shanksville, Pennsylvania.

10:28 a.m.
The North Tower of the World Trade Center collapses.

5:20 p.m.
Seven World Trade Center, a building just north of the Twin Towers, collapses.

CHAPTER FOUR

Building the Department

On January 24, 2003, Secretary Tom Ridge began his work combining more than 20 agencies from different departments into the Department of Homeland Security. He was now in charge of about 200,000 employees. The department's first budget was $37 billion.

In March, the agencies officially transferred to the DHS, coming from the FBI, Department of Energy, Department of Justice, Department of Health and Human Services, and more. The U.S. Coast Guard and Secret Service also joined the DHS, retaining their missions and reporting directly to Ridge.

The initial focus of the department was domestic terrorism prevention and response. One of its first projects was the launch of a website, Ready.gov. It was part of the Ready Campaign, which was aimed at providing citizens with tools and information to prepare for and respond to terrorist attacks and natural disasters until help arrived.

On March 17, 2003, the DHS launched Operation Liberty Shield with other departments in response to an elevated national threat level. This was a national plan to better protect infrastructure from attack and prepare citizens. The plan increased maritime and land border security, infrastructure protection, and airport and other transportation security.

Under Ridge's leadership, the DHS trained and placed airport screeners and increased the number of air marshals from 33 to more than 5,000. Ridge expanded the Container Security Initiative, which focused on the possible threats of maritime cargo containers. U.S. teams sent to ports around the world examined cargo containers considered to be high risk before they could proceed to the United States.

In 2003 several agencies, including the U.S. Coast Guard, were moved from other departments to the newly created DHS.

But the public criticized some of the department's first actions. When the threat level was raised to orange in February 2003, the DHS suggested citizens prepare an emergency supply kit in case of a terrorist attack. Among the list of items suggested for the kit were duct tape and plastic sheeting. Panicked Americans hurried to buy these items. Ridge had to calm their fears by stating that they did not need to rush to create safe rooms from the materials. The announcement was publicly ridiculed on talk shows. People wondered how duct tape and plastic sheeting could possibly protect them from an attack.

Creating the Department of Homeland Security had been difficult. One of its major problems was highlighted in the *9/11 Commission Report* released in 2004. This commission formed to investigate the causes for the 9/11 attacks and suggest ways to prepare for and respond to future terrorist attacks. The commission also investigated issues facing the DHS. It found that DHS leaders had to report to 88 Congressional committees. The report stated, "This is perhaps the single largest obstacle impeding the department's successful

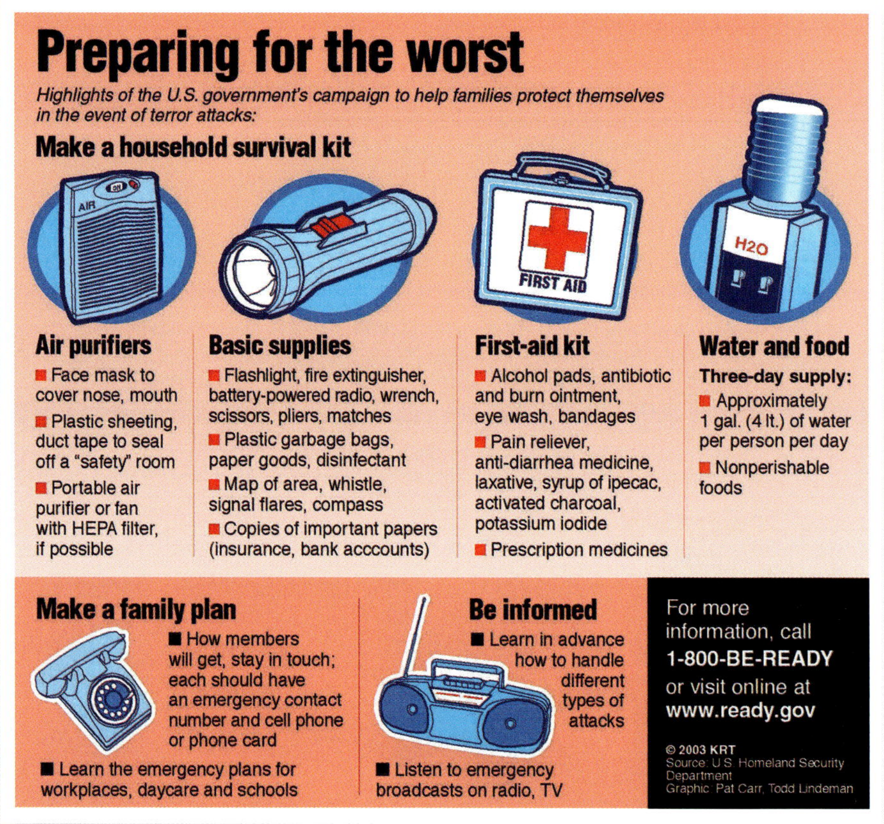

The DHS issued recommendations for supplies needed in the event of a terrorist attack, causing some public panic.

development." These committees review the work of the different agencies within the department, requiring huge amounts of time and effort for DHS leaders to prepare and present to the many different committees. Plus, the committees only offer advice based on a small part of the large department. Often one committee's advice isn't the same as another's. The entire review process is inefficient and continues to be a major challenge for the DHS.

Changes in Leadership

On November 30, 2004, Ridge announced he was leaving the DHS. His successor, Michael Chertoff, took office on February 15, 2005. Chertoff had been a federal judge and federal prosecutor who investigated cases involving terrorism, including the 9/11 attacks. As DHS secretary, he conducted a review of the department's organization, operations, and policies. He created a new agenda from its results. Some of his accomplishments as secretary were increasing airport and border security and focusing on disaster preparedness.

The department's response to natural disasters and Chertoff's leadership were tested in late August 2005. The most destructive hurricane in U.S. history, Hurricane Katrina, devastated coastal areas of Mississippi and Louisiana. Top wind speeds exceeded 125 miles (201 km) per hour. There were heavy rains. High floodbanks called levees broke. Seawater rushed into New Orleans and other cities. The flooding destroyed everything in sight. New Orleans was 80 percent underwater. More than 1,800 people died. The mayor ordered residents to leave the city, but thousands did not or could not. There was no response plan in place, no military help, no federal relief available immediately after the storm. People looted homes and businesses. They didn't have enough food and water. Many made their way to the Superdome or convention center, hoping to get food and shelter there while they waited to be evacuated. Many others climbed to the roofs of their apartments and homes, waiting to be rescued by helicopters.

FEMA, the DHS agency responsible for responding to natural disasters, was slow to provide the relief that the victims, the city of New Orleans, and the states of Louisiana and Mississippi needed. It was clear that FEMA and the state and local agencies it coordinated with were unprepared for this kind of disaster. People were suffering and dying as agencies figured out how to handle their response. A few days after the hurricane hit, Chertoff disregarded reports of thousands of people who didn't have food as merely being rumors.

New Orleans suffered massive flooding after Hurricane Katrina in 2005.

Many criticized Chertoff for his lack of leadership during the crisis. In response, he said, "I want to be clear, as the secretary of homeland security I am accountable and accept responsibility to the performance of the entire department, good and bad." The disaster showed FEMA's flaws and Chertoff promised to change the agency. In October 2006 President Bush signed the Post-Katrina Emergency Management Reform Act into law. It created new leadership positions and reorganized the agency so that it could respond better to future natural disasters.

The First Female Secretary

After Barack Obama became president in 2009, he chose the first female DHS secretary. Janet Napolitano was a former Arizona governor and attorney. Under her leadership, the DHS grew in several ways. In 2010 the DHS launched a new campaign with community involvement in national security. It was the "If You See Something, Say Something" campaign, adopted from the New York Metropolitan Transportation Authority. It encourages citizens to report to 9-1-1 any suspicious activity they see, such as someone who seems to be watching a building. While this could help the DHS find a terrorist planning an attack, it could also lead to racial profiling of Middle Eastern and Muslim people. In an effort to discourage this, the DHS website states, "Factors such as race, ethnicity, and/or religious affiliation are not suspicious. The public should only report suspicious behavior and situations."

Napolitano also enhanced airport security by creating the TSA precheck program. While the TSA had made traveling on airplanes safer, it led to long lines and waits at airports. The precheck program screens applicants. If it finds that a traveler is low risk, that person can pay a fee and use special precheck lines at airport checkpoints. The lines are faster, members do not need to remove their shoes, and they can leave liquids and electronics in their carry-on bags. Many people like and use the precheck program. But some groups who help protect privacy,

The phrase "If you see something, say something" became the slogan to get the public involved in reporting potential terrorist activity.

including the American Civil Liberties Union (ACLU), think the precheck program requires too much personal information from its applicants. They need to submit their height, weight, fingerprints, hair color, photograph, and more. TSA also is not required to explain why someone is declined for the program.

Immigration and Customs Enforcement is also part of the department. Napolitano led the creation of the Deferred Action for Childhood Arrivals (DACA) initiative in 2012. This program protected undocumented immigrants from being deported if they were brought into the country under the age of 16. The DACA program allowed its participants to get work permits so they could legally work in the United States and attend colleges. DACA participants are often called Dreamers.

An Evolving Department

When attorney Jeh Charles Johnson took over the secretary position in 2013, during Obama's second administration, the department had grown enormously since its beginning. The department now had 229,000 employees. The way terrorists worked had changed too. They used new strategies to find recruits, including using social media. While al-Qaeda lost some strength, a new radical Islamic terrorist group grew. ISIS formed from al-Qaeda in Iraq. It is based in Iraq and Syria. The terrorist group uses social media sites such as Twitter and Facebook to spread messages to its followers around the world. The new terrorists weren't all foreign-born visitors, as the September 11 hijackers had been. The DHS didn't need to stop these new terrorists from entering the United States. Many had lived here for years or even their entire lives. Terrorism was changing and the department had to change its antiterrorism efforts with it.

In response to the changing times, the DHS built tools they could use to search social media as part of their immigration vetting process. This process helps determine which immigrants can be allowed into the country. The department also hopes to find terrorist networks within the United States through social media postings and other evidence. Johnson also worked to improve the TSA, setting up a check system to ensure that agents would be able to find any suspicious materials in airport baggage. The National Terrorism Advisory System (NTAS) replaced the color-coded system introduced at the beginning of the department. It has two kinds of alerts: elevated and imminent. During Johnson's leadership, the DHS added a bulletin alert to the system in 2015, which advises the public about trends of terroristic threats.

President Obama appointed Jeh Johnson secretary of the DHS in 2013.

When President Donald J. Trump took office in 2017, he appointed John F. Kelly as the new DHS secretary. Kelly was in the position for just seven months. In late July he left the DHS to join Trump's administration as the chief of staff. Trump's new DHS secretary was the first DHS employee and second woman to be appointed to the position. Secretary Kirstjen M. Nielsen would lead the DHS into 2018.

Secretaries of Homeland Security

Tom Ridge
January 24, 2003–February 1, 2005

Michael Chertoff
February 15, 2005–January 21, 2009

Janet Napolitano
January 20, 2009–September 6, 2013

Jeh Charles Johnson
December 23, 2013–January 20, 2017

John F. Kelly
January 20, 2017–July 28, 2017

Kirstjen M. Nielsen
July 28, 2017–present

CHAPTER FIVE

Security Now and Into the Future

Protesters held signs saying "We Stand with Dreamers" and "No Person Is Illegal" as they crowded Capitol Hill in Washington, D.C., on March 5, 2018. It was a big day for the Deferred Action for Childhood Arrivals (DACA) program and Dreamers. Congress was supposed to decide how to handle the young undocumented immigrants protected by the program. President Trump had set the date six months earlier, when he decided to end the DACA program. He asked Congress to decide the fate of Dreamers by the March 5 deadline. Would Immigration and Customs Enforcement (ICE) deport them, or would the government allow them to stay in the United States?

For many Dreamers, the United States was the only home they'd ever known. Their parents brought them to the country as babies and young children. They had never been to the countries where they were born. Now they were living in limbo, unsure of their futures. As March 5 approached, Congress had no decision to give the 690,000 DACA recipients living in the United States. Trump had ordered March 5 to be the final date Dreamers could file for one final two-year renewal on their DACA permits. But several federal judges challenged Trump's DACA decision, ruling that the administration's decision was unlawful. Trump's administration appealed the rulings, but the courts hadn't come to a decision when the March 5 deadline arrived. The DHS still had to accept renewal applications from DACA recipients.

That decision left Dreamers uncertain of their futures. The protesters, Dreamers, and their allies who came from states around the country, wanted a decision. They wanted their voices heard and for Congress to act. One of those protestors was a man named Raul from Columbus, Nebraska. Raul said it was important for him to protest. "I think I am a Nebraskan. I've lived in Nebraska for 27 years and I think that as of now I don't see any other place that's my home than Nebraska. And if I were to be sent back or deported to Mexico—I don't know Mexico—Mexico is not my homeland anymore." Raul is one of many Dreamers facing possible deportations to countries they do not know.

Activists demonstrated in support of immigrants at a rally protesting President Trump's call to end DACA.

The outcome of DACA and the future of the Dreamers remains unknown. The Trump administration stays focused on immigration and border security. Dealing with the issue of DACA recipients and the program is just one of many issues facing Secretary Nielsen and the Department of Homeland Security.

Priorities in 2018

Nielsen and the DHS are focused on fulfilling the Trump administration's priorities related to homeland security. Regarding the DHS's missions of securing our borders and enforcing immigration laws, one of President Trump's big priorities is to build a border wall. The 1,954-mile (3,145-km) U.S.–Mexico border wall is Trump's proposal to help stop illegal immigration from Mexico. It was one of his biggest campaign promises. Trump also promised that Mexico would pay for its construction. This is a highly controversial issue. Its cost would be great, perhaps more than $21.6 billion. Its supporters believe that it would stop undocumented immigrants and the flow of illegal drugs from Central and South America into the United States. Others believe a border wall would be ineffective against drugs and illegal immigration. Illegal immigration is at its lowest point in four decades in the United States. Two-thirds of undocumented immigrants enter the country legally with a visa (a permit to stay in the country for a certain period of time) and then remain in the United States after their visas expire. Large areas of land along the border are privately owned. The government would have to purchase or seize the land from these people, which could be very costly. And much of the border is far from any nearby cities or roads, meaning that construction roads would have to be built first in order for construction to begin.

Congress has yet to approve funding for such a wall. Mexico refuses to pay for it. But the DHS is moving forward with the president's executive order issued on January 25, 2017. It requires the DHS to "take all appropriate steps to immediately plan, design, and construct a physical wall along the southern border,

Trump toured border wall prototypes in San Diego in 2018.

using appropriate materials and technology to most effectively achieve complete operational control of the southern border." In response, Customs and Border Protection had eight models of different kinds of walls built that could be used along the border. President Trump visited the models in March 2018. He said that a border wall is "truly the first line of defense." In addition to the border wall, the DHS is enforcing immigration laws through U.S. Immigration and Customs Enforcement (ICE). The DHS reported more than 226,000 deportations and 143,000 arrests of undocumented immigrants in 2017.

In its work toward the mission of preventing terrorism, the DHS began enhanced security screening measures for people entering the United States from the Trump administration's list of high-risk countries. These countries include Middle Eastern, Asian, and African nations: Egypt, Iran, Iraq, Libya, Mali, North Korea, Somalia, South Sudan, Sudan, Syria, and Yemen. The DHS believes this increased screening helps keep terrorists out of the country. As part of its airplane security efforts, the DHS temporarily banned electronic devices larger than cellphones from passenger cabins on flights headed to the U.S. from the Middle East and North Africa. In December 2017 Nielsen announced a new DHS office—the Countering Weapons of Mass Destruction Office. The office leads DHS efforts to stop terrorists from using weapons of mass destruction, whether they are biological, chemical, radiological, or nuclear weapons.

In response to the DHS's mission of disaster assistance, FEMA continues its work. The DHS reported it has provided $7.6 billion in disaster assistance since January 2017. During that time, the United States experienced three major hurricanes: Harvey, Irma, and Maria. California experienced wildfires and destructive mudslides.

Cybersecurity, one of the five primary DHS missions, continues to be a big issue for the department. Cyberattacks are when individuals or groups illegally gain access to others' computers and information technology. They can even hack into the computer systems of other countries. The DHS found that Russian hackers tried to access voter files and election sites during the U.S. 2016 presidential election. That's one of the ways foreign powers can now attack the United States.

The National Cybersecurity and Communications Integration Center in Arlington, Virginia, monitors for cyber threats.

Evolving Threats

So much has changed since the attacks of September 11, 2001. Before 9/11, the FAA, CIA, and FBI all had separate terrorist watch lists. That may be one of the reasons why two of the 9/11 hijackers, who were known terrorist suspects, were able to board the airplanes that killed close to 3,000 people. Today, security agencies share or access the same watch lists. Airplanes and airports are now more secure than they were before the attacks, making a repeat of 9/11 highly unlikely. But while U.S. homeland security has changed, terrorism has changed too. We are now prepared to prevent attacks of the kind that happened. But are the DHS and U.S. security agencies prepared for the attacks of the future?

While the DHS is working to protect U.S. borders to stop terrorists from entering the United States, new kinds of terrorism have emerged in the past 17 years. These are called "homegrown" and "lone wolf" terrorists. Homegrown terrorists do not come from another country. They are U.S. citizens or legal permanent residents. Some have been influenced by the messages and information terrorist groups from other countries post on social media. Lone wolf terrorists do not work with ISIS or al-Qaeda as part of a bigger plot to harm the U.S. They take inspiration from those organizations and act alone or with like-minded people. They do not communicate by phone or email with other terrorists, which could be tracked by national security agencies. They use encrypted computer code to spread and receive terrorist messages. ISIS is very skilled at using social media to spread its message.

The terrorist organization encourages small acts of terrorism using easily found weapons, such as knives, cars, and bombs made out of pressure cookers. Homegrown terrorists have been responsible for the biggest terrorist acts in the United States since 9/11. One of the worst happened on June 12, 2016, when American Omar Mateen opened fire in a nightclub that was a gathering spot for LGBTQ people in Orlando, Florida. He killed 49 people in the attack. He had pledged his allegiance to ISIS. Finding these kinds of terrorists is extremely difficult. They live quiet, seemingly normal lives but secretly ally themselves with ISIS.

In May 2017 the DHS issued a National Terrorism Advisory System bulletin describing the rising threat of homegrown terrorism. It stated that foreign terrorist organizations were continuing to use the Internet to inspire, enable, or direct people already living in the United States to commit terrorist acts. Bulletins like these help DHS in the fight to catch homegrown terrorists before they attack. The department describes the kinds of tactics ISIS encourages terrorists to use in their attacks. It urges people to report any suspicious activities they see.

TYPES OF ADVISORIES

Bulletin
Describes current developments or general trends regarding threats of terrorism.

Elevated Alert
Warns of a credible terrorism threat against the United States.

Imminent Alert
Warns of a credible, specific and impending terrorism threat against the United States.

The National Terrorism Advisory System has three warning levels: bulletin, elevated, and imminent.

Cybersecurity is a main focus of the DHS. Its National Cybersecurity and Communications Integration Center (NCCIC) tracks cyberattacks against government agencies and infrastructure. Its cyber detectives monitor government systems and Internet traffic looking for anything unusual. An increase in Internet traffic might mean cyberterrorists are trying to hack into a system.

DHS Secretary Nielsen and her successors in the DHS have some tough challenges ahead of them. As terrorism changes and border security remains a priority, the DHS will need to adapt along with the issues it faces. Nielsen is aware of the changing landscape of homeland security and believes that the DHS needs to make sure it's "addressing today's threat, and not yesterday's."

What You Can Do

If you're concerned about an issue that involves the Department of Homeland Security, you can write the lawmakers who represent you in Congress. Lawmakers can sometimes influence what the DHS does. This link will help you find the member of the House of Representatives for where you live:

https://www.house.gov/representatives/find-your-representative

This link shows the current members of the U.S. Senate. Each state has two senators:

https://www.senate.gov/senators/contact/

Timeline

September 11, 2001: Nineteen radical jihadist terrorists hijack four passenger airplanes, crashing two into the World Trade Center, one into the Pentagon, and another on a Pennsylvania field. The terrorist attacks were the work of al-Qaeda and they killed almost 3,000 people.

October 8, 2001: The Office of Homeland Security is created.

October 26, 2001: The PATRIOT Act passes, giving law enforcement agencies more surveillance powers.

November 19, 2001: The Aviation and Transportation Security Act passes, authorizing the creation of a new federal agency called the Transportation Security Administration (TSA).

March 2002: The Homeland Security Advisory Council is created.

June 2002: President George W. Bush submits his plan to Congress for the creation of a Department of Homeland Security (DHS).

November 2002: Congress passes the Homeland Security Act and President Bush signs it into law on November 25.

January 24, 2003: Tom Ridge becomes the first DHS secretary and begins his work to form the department.

March 2003: The more than 20 agencies that formed the DHS officially transfer to the department.

March 17, 2003: The DHS launches Operation Liberty Shield in conjunction with other departments in response to an elevated national threat level.

July 22, 2004: The 9/11 Commission releases its report on the causes of the 9/11 attacks and suggests ways to prevent future terrorist attacks.

February 15, 2005: Michael Chertoff becomes the second secretary of the DHS.

August 2005: Hurricane Katrina devastates parts of Mississippi and Louisiana. FEMA is slow to respond to the disaster and Chertoff is blamed for the agency's poorly planned relief.

October 2006: President Bush signs the Post-Katrina Emergency Management Reform Act into law, establishing new FEMA leadership positions and reorganizing the agency so that it can better respond to future natural disasters.

January 20, 2009: President Barack Obama appoints Janet Napolitano as the third secretary of the DHS.

July 1, 2010: The DHS launches the "If You See Something, Say Something" campaign, urging Americans to report suspicious activity related to terrorism to local law enforcement.

May 2, 2011: U.S. Special Forces find and kill al-Qaeda leader Osama bin Laden, the man who orchestrated the 9/11 attacks.

June 15, 2012: President Barack Obama announces the Deferred Action for Childhood Arrivals (DACA) initiative to protect certain undocumented immigrants who entered the country as children from being deported and allow them to legally work through work permits.

December 23, 2013: Jeh Johnson becomes the fourth secretary of the DHS.

January 20, 2017: President Donald Trump appoints John Kelly as the fifth secretary of the DHS.

September 5, 2017: The Trump Administration announces the end of DACA and orders the DHS to stop accepting renewal applications from its recipients.

December 6, 2017: Kirstjen Nielsen becomes the sixth secretary of the DHS.

Glossary

ballistic missile—an airborne weapon that launches through rocket power and then falls through the force of gravity to hit its target

civil defense—training and organizing citizens to prepare for and protect themselves during wartime

cyberspace—the online environment of computer networks and the Internet

cyberterrorism—the use of computers and computer networks to disrupt infrastructure and vital processes of a country

evacuation—the removal of people from a dangerous area

hijacker—someone who unlawfully takes control of a vehicle, such as an airplane

infrastructure—the public works of a country, such as bridges, electricity grids, and dams

jihadist—a person who participates in or supports a holy war in the name of Islam

LGBTQ—lesbian, gay, bisexual, transgender, queer or questioning

terrorist—a person who uses violence to kill, injure, or make people and governments afraid

vulnerability—a quality that exposes a country to the possibility of attack

Additional Resources

Critical Thinking

1. In Chapter 2 the author describes the history of civil defense in the United States, including the invention of airplanes. How do you think that the invention of airplanes influenced the country's need for civil defense? Why do you think that? Support your reasoning with a quote from the text.

2. Chapter 3 begins with a narrative description of the events that unfolded on the morning of 9/11 from the perspective of the average American watching television. Why do you think the author chose this way to open the chapter on the creation of the Department of Homeland Security?

3. In the sidebar titled *Duck and Cover*, the author describes a propaganda video made for children by the U.S. government in the 1950s. Read the description and lyrics and then watch the video here: https://www.youtube.com/watch?v=IKqXu-5jw60. What information can you gather from the video that the text does not describe? Summarize the information from both sources. How are they different? How are they similar?

Further Reading

Green, Robert. *Debates on the 9/11 Attacks.* San Diego, CA: ReferencePoint Press, Inc., 2019.

Nardo, Don. *Ground Zero: How a Photograph Sent a Message of Hope.* North Mankato, MN: Capstone Press, 2017.

Peters, Jennifer. *Inside the Department of Homeland Security.* New York: Enslow Publishing, 2019.

Woog, Adam. *Careers in Homeland Security.* New York: Cavendish Square Publishing, 2014.

Internet Sites

Use Facthound to find Internet sites related to this book.

Visit www.facthound.com

Just type in 9780756559014 and go.

Source Notes

p. 4, "BALLISTIC MISSILE THREAT INBOUND . . . " Adam Nagourney, David E. Sanger and Johanna Barr. "Hawaii Emergency Management Agency." *The New York Times*. 13 Jan. 2018. https://www.nytimes.com/2018/01/13/us/hawaii-missile.html Accessed on July 15, 2018.

p. 4, "If you are outdoors, seek . . ." Associated Press and CBS. "Hawaii missile alert: False alarm warns residents of "ballistic missile threat" CBS. 13 Jan. 2018. https://www.cbsnews.com/news/hawaii-missile-alert-emergency-management-system-false-ballistic-missile-warning-2018-1-13/ Accessed on July 15, 2018.

p. 4, "a nuclear button is always on my desk ..." Mac William Bishop, Bruce Harrison, and Lauren Suk. "North Korea, South Korea could meet for talks ahead of Olympics." NBC News. 2 Jan. 2018. https://www.nbcnews.com/news/north-korea/north-korea-south-korea-could-meet-talks-ahead-olympics-n833941 Accessed on July 15, 2018.

p. 5, "I was sitting in the bathtub . . ." Adam Nagourney, David E. Sanger and Johanna Barr. "Hawaii Panics After Alert About Incoming Missile Is Sent in Error." *The New York Times*. 13 Jan. 2018. https://www.nytimes.com/2018/01/13/us/hawaii-missile.html Accessed on July 15, 2018.

p. 16, "Never in our history has the civilian . . ." Patrick S. Roberts. *Disasters and the American State*. New York: Cambridge University Press, 50.

p. 18, "the basic framework for preparations to . . ." Harry S. Truman Presidential Library & Museum. "Statement by the President Upon Signing the Federal Civil Defense Act of 1950." 12 Jan. 1951. https://www.trumanlibrary.org/publicpapers/index.php?pid=210 Accessed September 22, 2018.

p. 19, "There was a turtle by the name of Bert . . ." "Duck And Cover (1951) Bert The Turtle." YouTube, Nuclear Vault. https://www.youtube.com/watch?v=IKqXu-5jw60 Accessed on July 15, 2018.

p. 26, "America was targeted for attack because . . ." George W. Bush. "Address to the Nation on the Terrorist Attacks." September 11, 2001. The American Presidency Project. http://www.presidency.ucsb.edu/ws/index.php?pid=58057 Accessed on July 15, 2018.

p. 34, "Jewish-Christian" Dominic Tierney. "The Twenty Years' War." *The Atlantic*. 23 Aug. 2016. https://www.theatlantic.com/international/archive/2016/08/twenty-years-war/496736/ Accessed on July 15, 2018.

p. 40-41, "This is perhaps the single largest obstacle . . ." "The 9/11 Commission Report." 421. http://govinfo.library.unt.edu/911/report/911Report.pdf Accessed on July 15, 2018.

p. 43, "I want to be clear, as the secretary . . ." Associated Press. "Chertoff overhauls FEMA, rejects criticism." NBC News. 13 Feb. 2006. http://www.nbcnews.com/id/11325036/ns/us_news-katrina_the_long_road_back/t/chertoff-overhauls-fema-rejects-criticism/#.WsUk5K25Bt8 Accessed on July 15, 2018.

p. 43, "Factors such as race, ethnicity . . ." "If You See Something, Say Something." Department of Homeland Security. https://www.dhs.gov/see-something-say-something/what-suspicious-activity Accessed on July 15, 2018.

p. 49, "I think I am a Nebraskan . . ." Cheyenne Haslett. "Dreamers protest on Capitol Hill on DACA deadline day." ABCNews. 5 March 2018. Video: 6:40-7:25. http://abcnews.go.com/Politics/dreamers-protest-capitol-hill-daca-deadline-day/story?id=53539262 Accessed on July 15, 2018.

p. 50-52, "take all appropriate steps to immediately . . ." "Executive Order: Border Security and Immigration Enforcement Improvements." The White House. 25 Jan. 2017. https://www.whitehouse.gov/presidential-actions/executive-order-border-security-immigration-enforcement-improvements/ Accessed on July 15, 2018.

p. 52, "truly the first line of defense . . ." Dartunorro Clark. "Trump visits California to see wall prototypes near Mexico border." NBC News. 13 Mar 2018. https://www.nbcnews.com/politics/white-house/trump-visits-california-see-wall-prototypes-near-mexico-border-n854836 Accessed on July 15, 2018.

p. 56, "addressing today's threat . . ." Meredith Somers. "Nominee for DHS secretary promises employee protection, border and information security." Federal News Radio. 8 Nov. 2017. https://federalnewsradio.com/management/2017/11/nominee-for-dhs-secretary-promises-employee-protection-border-and-information-security-under-her-watch/ Accessed on July 15, 2018.

Select Bibliography

"The 9/11 Commission Report." http://govinfo.library.unt.edu/911/report

Brill, Steven. "Are We Any Safer?" *The Atlantic*. September 2016.

Bush, George W. "Address to the Nation on the Terrorist Attacks." September 11, 2001. The American Presidency Project. Web. http://www.presidency.ucsb.edu/ws/index.php?pid=58057 Accessed on July 15, 2018.

Bush, George W. "The Department of Homeland Security." June 2002. https://www.dhs.gov/sites/default/files/publications/book_0.pdf Accessed on July 15, 2018.

Calabresi, Massimo. "Homeland security, ISIS and the fight against fear." *TIME*. 2015. 48-52.

The Department of Homeland Security website: https://www.dhs.gov/ Accessed on July 15, 2018.

Haynes, Wendy. "Seeing around Corners: Crafting the New Department of Homeland Security." *Review of Policy Research*, Volume 21, Number 3 (2004).

Homeland Security National Preparedness Task Force. "Civil Defense and Homeland Security: A Short History of National Preparedness Efforts." September 2006.

Nemeth, Charles P. *Homeland Security: An Introduction to Principles and Practice*. Boca Raton, FL: Auerbach Publications, 2010.

Index

About the Author

Karen Latchana Kenney writes books about nature, biodiversity, conservation, scientific discoveries, historical events, and more. Born in New Amsterdam, Guyana, she moved to Minnesota at a young age and began writing in elementary school. Her award-winning and star-reviewed books include *Exoplanets: Worlds beyond Our Solar System*; *Everything World War I*; and *TV Brings Battle into the Home with the Vietnam War*. She lives in Minneapolis with her husband and son, and she bikes, hikes, and gazes at the night sky in northern Minnesota any moment she can. Visit her online at http://latchanakenney.wordpress.com.